The Red Badge of Courage

STEPHEN CRANE

Level 3

Retold by Mary Gladwin
Series Editors: Andy Hopkins and Jocelyn Potter

Pearson Education Limited
Edinburgh Gate, Harlow,
Essex CM20 2JE, England
and Associated Companies throughout the world.

ISBN 0 582 42126 8

First published in the USA by D. Appleton & Company 1895
First published by Penguin Books 1983
This edition first published 2000

Text copyright © Penguin Books 2000
Illustrations copyright © Gino D'Achille (Artist Partners) 2000

Typeset by Digital Type, London
Set in 11/14pt Bembo
Printed in Spain by Mateu Cromo, S. A. Pinto (Madrid)

Published by Pearson Education Limited in association with
Penguin Books Ltd, both companies being subsidiaries of Pearson Plc

For a complete list of the titles available in the Penguin Readers series please write to your local
Pearson Education office or to: Marketing Department, Penguin Longman Publishing,
5 Bentinck Street, London W1M 5RN.

Contents

		page
Introduction		v
Chapter 1	"I'm tired of waiting!"	1
Chapter 2	"We're leaving!"	4
Chapter 3	"When are we going to fight?"	7
Chapter 4	"They're coming!"	12
Chapter 5	"They're coming again!"	16
Chapter 6	"Where's your wound?"	20
Chapter 7	"Leave me alone!"	24
Chapter 8	"Don't try to stop me!"	28
Chapter 9	"I'll look after you"	33
Chapter 10	"They fight like cowboys!"	37
Chapter 11	"Give it to me!"	42
Chapter 12	"He's wrong!"	46
Chapter 13	"It's finished!"	50
Activities		54

Introduction

There was a loud shout: "Forward, march!" They heard the sound of marching feet as another regiment passed. They followed them into the dark in two long blue lines. They heard more men marching behind them. All that day, the army marched under a clear blue sky. They passed over hills and through woods.

The young soldier walked along, saying nothing. He looked around nervously. "What's that noise?" he asked himself. "Is it gunfire? And is that smoke?"

This is the story of a young American soldier named Henry Fleming. When he is a boy, he dreams of going to war. He thinks that war is an adventure. He wants to be a hero.

When he is older, his country is at war. The north of the country is fighting against the south. Everyone is always talking about the war. The newspapers are full of stories about great battles. Henry leaves home and joins the army. When he puts on his new uniform, he feels proud and excited. He is ready to fight for his part of the country, the North.

He quickly discovers that a soldier's life isn't always exciting. He spends many months in an army camp. He and the other new soldiers learn to march and to shoot. Henry has a lot of time to think. He asks himself what he will do in a battle. Will he run or fight? Is he as brave as the other men? He won't know the answers until the fighting starts.

After some time, the regiment faces the enemy. Henry and the other new soldiers are tested. They measure their courage against the enemy, their comrades, and themselves. Some are braver than others. Henry tries to understand the reasons. Maybe they are stronger than the others. Maybe they don't understand the danger. Some soldiers try to help their comrades. Others only help themselves. Who is right and who is wrong?

The war is seen through Henry's eyes, but he is like every other young soldier. He is fighting in the American Civil War, but it is like every other war.

The American Civil War was fought from 1861 to 1865, between the North and the South of the United States of America. The two parts of the country were very different. In the South, the main activity was farming. In the North, there were many big cities and factories. The war started when the states of the South wanted to leave the United States of America.

About two million men fought in the war for the North, and about 900,000 men fought for the South. Many of the battles were fought in the South. A lot of this part of the country was destroyed.

In *The Red Badge of Courage*, Henry belongs to a Northern regiment. The battle in this book is like the Battle of Chancellorsville. That was fought in Virginia in May 1863. There were around 130,000 men fighting for the North and 60,000 for the South. Many men were killed or wounded on both sides. The South won the battle, but they later lost the war.

The writer of this book, Stephen Crane, was born in New Jersey in 1871. He was the youngest child in a family of fourteen children.

In 1890, he went to New York and began writing for a newspaper. He lived in a poor area of the city. He wrote about the people that he met there. In 1893, his first book came out. It was called *Maggie, A Girl of the Streets*. He continued working for other newspapers after this.

The Red Badge of Courage came out in 1895, and it made Stephen Crane famous. Many people thought that Crane fought in the Civil War. They didn't know that he was born after the war. He was never a soldier, but he described a soldier's life very well. This book is very different from other books that were written at this time. Crane wrote about the fear and suffering of ordinary soldiers. In his book, they aren't always heroes, and war is not just an adventure.

Because of this book, Crane was able to work for other American and foreign newspapers. In 1896, he traveled by ship from the United States to Cuba. The ship was destroyed, and he escaped in a small boat. He became very ill as a result. Two years later, he wrote a story about his escape. The book was called *The Open Boat and Other Stories.*

Stephen Crane went to live in England in 1897, and he became friends with other famous writers there. He continued to travel and to write for newspapers. He wrote about the war between Greece and Turkey in 1897. He also wrote about the Spanish–American War in 1898. He wrote two books of poems, *The Black Riders and Other Lines* (1895) and *War is Kind and Other Poems* (1899). His other books are *Active Service* (1899), *Whilomville Stories* (1900) and *Wounds in the Rain* (1900).

Stephen Crane died in Germany in 1900 at the age of twenty-eight.

Chapter 1   "I'm tired of waiting!"

In the cold early morning, the army was slowly waking up. It was resting in some green hills. A wide brown river lay at its feet. Across the river shone the red eyes of the enemy's fires.

A tall soldier ran up from the river. "We're going to move tomorrow!" he shouted. Men in blue uniforms came closer to listen. "We're going to attack the enemy!"

"That's a lie!" said one soldier loudly. "We're not going to move!"

"It's true!" said the tall soldier. "I heard it from a friend, and he heard it from his brother. And his brother heard it from an officer."

"We can't move!" said a young officer. "I've just put a new floor in my tent. It's made of wood, and it cost a lot of money!"

Groups of men talked excitedly. Some of them believed the tall soldier, but some of them had other ideas. One young soldier listened without speaking. Then he went into his tent. He wanted to be alone and to think.

"Are we really going to fight tomorrow?" he asked himself. "What will happen to me?"

◆

When he was a boy, he dreamed of war. In his dreams, he was a hero, fighting for his country and its people. Then when he was older, his country was at war. The newspapers told stories of great battles. He wanted to join the brave soldiers in the blue army because he didn't want to miss this adventure.

His mother was against the idea. "Don't be stupid, Henry," she said. "Why do you want to go? A soldier's life is hard. You don't know what it's like. I don't want you to get hurt. I need you here on the farm more than the army needs you."

"We're going to attack the enemy!"

He continued to read the newspapers. There was fine fighting down there. He talked to the people in the town. "We're winning!" they said. "Our boys in blue are doing a wonderful job!"

When he heard this, he couldn't wait. He got up early one morning and went into town. He came back wearing a blue uniform. "I've joined the army," he told his mother excitedly.

She didn't look up. "I see," she said quietly. There were tears in her eyes. She helped him pack his bags. "I put some new socks and your best shirts into your bag," she said. "You'll always be warm. And choose your friends carefully. There are a lot of bad men in the army. Remember your father. He never drank and he never used bad language. So be careful and be a good boy."

Henry listened to his mother impatiently. Then, when she finished, he left. He turned back to say a last goodbye. He saw his mother crying.

He went into town to say goodbye to his friends. He felt proud in his new blue uniform. Young girls smiled at him and old men waved. He felt like a hero already.

After a long trip by train, he arrived in the camp by the river.

♦

"We've been here for months," he thought. "We've practiced firing our rifles. And we've marched. And we've practiced and marched again. I'm tired of waiting! Are we ever going to fight?"

The men sat and told stories. The older soldiers laughed at the new ones. They shouted at them when they passed: "Fresh fish!" They all waited together. They didn't know why.

The young soldier saw the enemy once or twice. He was guarding one side of the stream, and they were guarding the other. He spoke to a small, thin man in gray. He liked him. "You're a good man," said the gray soldier. Henry felt sorry that they were at war.

The older soldiers told terrible stories about the enemy soldiers. "There are thousands and thousands of them," they said. "They're strong and they're hungry. Nothing can stop them!" They talked about the smoke, fire, and blood of battle.

Henry didn't always believe them. "They're lying," he told himself. "They're just trying to scare the new soldiers."

He suddenly felt afraid as he imagined his first battle. "Will I fight like a hero?" he asked himself. "Or will I run away?"

The tall soldier came into the tent, followed by the loud soldier. They were still talking angrily. "You'll see! There'll be a big battle tomorrow, I'm sure!" said the tall soldier.

The young soldier looked at him. "Jim, do you think the regiment will fight very well?"

"They'll fight all right when they start shooting," replied the tall soldier calmly.

The young soldier continued, "Do you think any of the boys will run away?"

The tall soldier thought for a minute. "Maybe a few of them will run when the fighting starts. They're a new regiment, so you never know. I think they'll fight as well as the others."

"And you, Jim?" asked the young soldier. "Do you think you'll run?"

"Maybe I'll run if the others run," he replied. "But if the others fight, I'll fight with them."

"You don't know what you'll do!" said the loud soldier.

But Henry wasn't listening. "I'm glad Jim said that," he said to himself. "I'm not the only one who's scared."

Chapter 2   "We're leaving!"

The next morning, the young soldier learned that the tall soldier was wrong. The army didn't move the next day, or the next, but

4

stayed in the camp. Henry had time to think. And he had time to worry.

He listened to his comrades talking excitedly about the battle. "Aren't they afraid?" he asked himself. "Maybe they're braver than I am. Or maybe they're just hiding their fear." He began to feel angry with himself. He was also angry with the generals. "Why don't we move? What are they waiting for?"

Then, early one morning, the young soldier woke up to the sound of loud voices: "Get up! We're leaving!"

It was still dark as he joined the other soldiers. They formed a line, carrying their rifles and equipment. They could see the red fires of the enemy camp across the river. They stood waiting for a long time.

Finally, an officer on horseback arrived with their orders. There was a loud shout: "Forward, march!" They heard the sound of marching feet as another regiment passed. They followed them into the dark in two long blue lines. They heard more men marching behind them. All that day, the army marched under a clear blue sky. They passed over hills and through woods.

The young soldier walked along, saying nothing. He looked around nervously. "What's that noise?" he asked himself. "Is it gunfire? And is that smoke?"

He looked into the faces of his comrades. He was hoping to see fear and worry. To his surprise, they were excited and happy. Some were discussing the army's plans for them.

The tall soldier was speaking. "You see? We're moving away from the river. We're going to come in behind the enemy lines."

"He's right!" said another man. "I had the same idea!"

Other voices spoke. "Me too!"

Not everyone agreed. "You're all crazy!" said a loud voice. "You don't know where we're going!"

Other men were laughing and joking. Henry didn't join in their conversations or their jokes. He felt sad and alone.

A fat soldier tried to steal a horse from a farmyard. He wanted it to carry his bag. He was escaping with his prize, when a young girl ran out from the farmhouse. She pulled the horse by the head and the fat soldier pulled on the other side.

The regiment stopped. They called to the young girl: "Hit him with a stick!" They laughed at the fat soldier as he returned to the line with his bag. They waved happily to the girl as they continued their march. They forgot the war for a few minutes.

In the evening, the line broke into regiments again. The regiments went into the fields to make camp. Soon there were tents and campfires on all sides.

The young soldier left his camp and walked into the quiet night. He lay down in the soft grass. He looked at the moon shining through the trees. He felt very lonely. "Why did I leave home?" he thought. He missed the farm. He thought about the fields and the house. "That's where I belong. I'm not a soldier. I'm not like the others."

He heard a noise in the grass and saw the loud soldier. "Wilson!" he called.

The loud soldier came near and looked down. "Hello, Henry. Is it you? What are you doing here?"

"Oh, just thinking," replied the young soldier.

The other man sat down and lit his pipe. "You don't look very happy," he said. "What's wrong?"

"Oh, nothing," replied Henry.

The loud soldier started talking about the battle. "This time we're really going to fight!" he said. His voice was happy and excited. "And we're going to beat them! I'm sure we're going to win!" He became more serious. "They've beaten us every time until now, but this time, we'll win!"

"But you think this march is stupid, don't you?" asked the young soldier.

"No," explained the other man. "I'm happy to march if we

fight at the end. But I hate moving around for no reason. And we're tired and the food is bad!"

"Jim says we're going to fight this time," said the young soldier.

"He's right," said the loud soldier. His voice grew excited again and he jumped to his feet. "And we're going to win, I'm sure!" He spoke like an old soldier.

The young soldier looked at him coldly. "Oh, you're going to do great things, I guess!"

"Oh, I don't know. But I'll fight as well as other men!" replied the loud soldier.

"How do you know that you won't run away?" asked the young soldier.

"Run away? Me? Of course not!"

The young soldier continued, "But you're not the bravest man in the world, are you?"

"I didn't say that!" The loud soldier was angry. "And who are you? Why did you ask me a question like that?" He walked away, leaving Henry alone again.

Henry slowly returned to his tent and lay down next to the sleeping tall soldier. He stayed awake for a long time. He asked himself the same painful questions again and again: "Will I be brave? Or will I run away?" At last, he fell into a deep sleep.

Chapter 3   "When are we going to fight?"

The new regiment marched all the next day. They crossed a bridge over the river, and then they camped near a forest. The young soldier was afraid of the forest. "Maybe the enemy's hiding there!" he thought. "Maybe they're going to attack us in the dark!" He watched the forest carefully, but he saw nothing.

Early the next morning, they followed a narrow road into the forest. They marched for hours without stopping.

Early the next morning, they followed a narrow road into the forest.

"I'm tired!" said the loud soldier unhappily. "And my feet hurt!"

"My bag's too heavy," said the tall soldier. "I'm going to leave it here." He put it down by the side of the road.

The other soldiers did the same. They left everything that they didn't need. Each man kept only his clothes, bed cover, food, water, rifle, and bullets. "You can eat and shoot now," said the tall soldier. "That's all that you need to do."

The new regiment could now move more quickly, like the older regiments. They still looked like a new regiment, though. Their uniforms were still new, and the colors of their flag were still bright.

Finally, the army sat down to rest. "This isn't a real war. We're just practicing," thought Henry. "We're just marching and marching. When are we going to fight?"

Then, one gray morning, the army began to run. The young soldier was not really awake, but he had to run with his comrades. He was afraid of falling. "The others will run over me!" he thought. He was carried along by the crowd. For a second he felt as weak as a baby. The skin that covered his heart seemed very thin.

He took the time to look around him. He could not stop and he could not escape from the regiment. It was all around him. The laws and the history of his country were on four sides. He was in a moving box. He felt very afraid. "I never wanted to fight in the war," he told himself. "The government brought me here. And now I'm going to die!"

The regiment crossed a little stream. Suddenly, the young soldier heard the sound of cannon fire in front of him. He forgot his fear and ran faster. He only wanted to see the fighting. His heart was beating very quickly as he climbed up a hill.

He was surprised when he looked down. There wasn't a big battlefield. There were some small green fields with trees all around them. Small groups of soldiers were running through the trees and firing their rifles. A dark battle line of soldiers lay on the grass. A flag waved brightly.

The regiment formed into a battle line and began to move toward the woods. Henry watched the soldiers who were firing busily. "What are they firing at?" he asked himself. "I can't see anything."

Just then, he saw a dead soldier lying on the ground. He wore broken shoes and an old brown uniform that was too big for him. The young soldier looked into his face with great interest. "He fought and he died," he thought. "He knows what it's like. But he can't tell me."

After that, he didn't want to see the battle. When he was running up the hill, he was ready to fight. Now he had time to think. He was afraid again. His back felt cold and his legs felt weak. He saw danger all around him. The shadows in the woods looked like enemy soldiers. "We can't go in there!" he told himself. "They'll kill us all!"

He looked at his comrades. They were walking calmly through fields and woods. Their faces showed interest but not fear. They wanted to see their first battle.

The young soldier wanted to shout at them, "Stop! Go back! We're all going to die! Don't you understand?" He opened his mouth, but he couldn't make a sound. He was too afraid. "They'll laugh at me if I tell them to go back," he thought. "They won't understand. They're too stupid. I'm the only one who understands. And nobody will believe me."

He felt very sorry for himself. He walked slowly, with his head down. A young officer saw him, and started beating him on the shoulder with his sword. "Hurry, young man!" he said in a loud voice. "Hurry!"

The young soldier walked faster, but he kept his head down. He hated the young officer. "He doesn't understand me!" he told himself angrily. "Stupid animal!"

The regiment continued marching. After some time, they stopped in a large, open space in a forest. They could still hear the sound of rifle fire. They could see little balls of white smoke from the rifles.

Many men in the regiment began to build little hills in front of them, using earth, stones, and sticks. They wanted to protect themselves against the enemy bullets. But then the regiment was ordered to move. The young soldier was very surprised. "Why did we come here?" he asked the tall soldier. "Why are we leaving so soon?"

"I'm sure there's a good reason," replied the tall soldier patiently.

They moved to a new position, and they built more little hills. Then they moved again. And again. The loud soldier was angry. "When are we going to fight?" he cried. "What's the purpose of all this marching? Those generals are stupid!"

Now the tall soldier was angry. "Be quiet!" he shouted. "You're not a general!"

"I just want to fight," explained the loud soldier. "I didn't come here to walk!"

The regiment marched into the forest. Henry began to worry again. "Will I be brave, or will I run away?" he asked himself. He thought about dying, and a new idea came to him. "If I die, I'll be able to rest." He began to feel less afraid.

Just then, he heard the sound of cannon fire. He saw a group of soldiers running and firing. He heard the sound of their rifles. The regiment on his right was standing and firing all together. He watched them through a cloud of smoke. The noise grew louder.

Suddenly, he felt a heavy hand on his shoulder. It was the loud soldier. "It's my first and last battle," he said sadly. "I'm sure that I'm going to die." He had tears in his eyes and his hands were shaking. He gave the young soldier a small package in a yellow envelope. "There are some letters inside. I want you to give them to my family."

"What do you mean?" cried Henry. But there was no reply. The other soldier walked away.

Chapter 4   "They're coming!"

Henry's regiment stopped outside a wood. Through the trees, they could see some open fields and a thick cloud of smoke. In the smoke they could see a line of men running toward them. A team of horses ran with the men, pulling cannon on wheels.

A shell screamed over their heads and landed in the woods near them. A cloud of brown earth flew up into the air and showered down on them. Bullets hit the trees where they were hiding. The soldiers stayed very close to the ground.

They heard a loud cry of pain. A young officer was shot in the hand. Another officer covered his wound with a clean piece of cloth.

Far away, the battle flag was falling, and there was smoke and fire all around. Men in blue came out of the smoke, running like wild horses. More and more men ran toward the regiment, shouting. Their voices mixed with the sound of the bullets and the shells. As they came closer, the older regiments began to laugh at them. "What's the matter? What are you afraid of?" they called. "Are you trying to hide?"

Officers on horseback were beating them with their swords and kicking them. "Stop! Go back!" they cried. The running men didn't see or hear them.

Henry saw the fear on their faces. He wanted to run, but he couldn't. His legs refused to move. "What are they running from?" he asked himself. "I want to see it. But when I see it, maybe I'll run too!"

The young soldier only had to wait for a few minutes.

"They're coming!" cried a voice.

The men checked their rifles. Henry had a terrible thought: "Is there a bullet in my rifle?"

A general stopped his horse near another officer on horseback. "You have to stop them!" he shouted angrily.

"Yes, General," the officer replied nervously. "We'll try!"

The man next to the young soldier was talking to himself: "Oh, no, we're in trouble now!"

A young officer stood at the back of the regiment. "Don't fire, boys! Wait until I tell you! Wait until they come close!"

Suddenly, a crowd of enemy soldiers came running across the field, shouting wildly. The young soldier didn't have time to think. He threw his rifle into position and fired a first wild shot. He immediately began to work like a machine. He put in another bullet. He fired his rifle, again and again. He suddenly forgot about himself. He was part of the regiment and part of the army. His country was in danger, and he had to protect it.

He knew that his comrades were all around him. They were all brothers, fighting the same enemy. They all faced the danger of death. He could see them through the smoke. They reached down to get another bullet. Then they stood up to fire. He could hear the sound of metal on metal as they put in the bullets. The rifles made a loud crashing noise. Strange sounds came from the soldiers' mouths. Some shouted and some sang. Some made noises like wild animals. The tall soldier cursed.

The officers stayed behind the soldiers, shouting orders. They watched the enemy through the thick smoke. A man dropped his rifle. He ran away, screaming. An officer stopped him and began hitting him. He pushed him back toward the line. The man looked at the officer with the eyes of a beaten dog. He tried to put a bullet into his rifle, but his hands were shaking. The officer helped him.

He fought against the enemy soldiers.

The young soldier's mouth was dry and his eyes felt like hot stones. The noise of the guns filled his ears and the smoke burned his nose. He fought against the pain and the smoke while he fought against the enemy soldiers. He was angry with his rifle, because it fired only one bullet at a time. He wanted to run forward and kill everyone.

The man next to him fell to the ground. Blood poured from his chest. A bullet touched one soldier on the side of his head. He dropped his rifle and held his head in his hands. Then he ran. Another man had a bullet in his knee. He sat against a tree, crying, "Help me, help me!" The young officer was killed early in the battle. He lay on the ground like a tired man, but there was a surprised look on his face.

The young soldier heard loud shouting along the line. The blue soldiers stopped firing. As the smoke slowly cleared, he saw small groups of men in brown running away. One man turned around to fire a last shot. Then he disappeared into the smoke.

Some of the men began to shout happily. Many others were silent, thinking. The young soldier felt hot and dirty, and very thirsty. He sat down, and took a long drink of warm water. He heard excited voices around him: "We did it! We stopped them!"

He looked around, happy to be alive. Dead men were lying on the ground where they fell. Their arms and legs were in strange positions. A line of wounded men walked slowly past him.

Suddenly, he heard a loud crash behind him. He saw a line of cannon and busy soldiers. They were firing shells over his head into the enemy lines. He heard shouts and rifle fire coming from a hillside. He saw flags waving in the smoke, and he felt proud. "Our boys are still fighting!" he thought. Then he looked up. The sky was blue, and the sun was shining on the trees and fields. "It's so beautiful here," he thought, "even when there's a war."

Chapter 5 "They're coming again!"

The young soldier stood up slowly. "It's finished!" he said to himself happily. "The battle is finished! And I'm a real soldier now." He was very proud of himself. He smiled at his comrades.

"It's hot, isn't it?" he said.

"You're right! It's too hot for fighting!" was the reply.

He shook hands and spoke with the other soldiers. After the battle, they were all his friends and his brothers.

Just then, he heard cries of surprise along the line. "They're coming again!"

A crowd of enemy soldiers ran out of the woods. The shells flew over their heads again, and broke into pieces in the grass. They looked like strange war flowers.

The tired regiment slowly moved into position. "No! Not again!" one man cried. "We're too tired!"

Henry looked at the running men. "Who are they? Are they men or machines?" he asked himself. He slowly lifted his rifle and fired it into the crowded field. He looked again through the smoke. More and more soldiers were running toward him, shouting loudly. "They're too strong for us! We can't beat them!" he thought. He closed his eyes, waited and listened.

A soldier near him stopped firing. He threw down his rifle and ran away screaming. One after another, the soldiers dropped their rifles and ran. The young soldier opened his eyes. He was alone. He turned his head and saw his comrades disappearing into the smoke. He was lost. He didn't know which way to run. There was danger on all sides. Suddenly, he began to run away from the battlefield. He dropped his rifle. His open coat flew in the wind.

He passed a young officer. "Stop! Go back!" the officer cried. He hit a running man with his sword, but the man ran faster.

The young soldier ran without seeing. Two or three times he

The young soldier ran without seeing.

fell down. Once he knocked his shoulder heavily against a tree. He could still hear gunfire. He felt more and more afraid because he couldn't see the battle. When he was fighting, he was facing the enemy. Now the enemy was behind him and he imagined a bullet in his back.

He noticed that he wasn't alone. There were running men on his right and on his left, and he heard footsteps behind him. All the regiment was running away. The crashing sounds of battle followed them. Henry was glad that there were men behind him. He knew that the danger was behind them. "They'll die first," he told himself. "If I stay at the front, I'll be safe." He ran faster and stayed at the front of the group.

The young soldier ran across a little field, followed by his comrades. Shells flew over their heads, screaming. One landed near him and knocked him to the ground. He wasn't hurt. He jumped up and continued running. He was surprised to see a line of six cannon. Soldiers were firing shells at the enemy position. They fired and fired again like machines. Henry felt sorry for them. He wanted to shout at them, "Run! The enemy's coming!" But he said nothing, and continued running. He knew that they were dead men.

He climbed a little hill. Far away, he saw a bright flag waving. A regiment was running to help its comrades. "What kind of men are they?" he asked himself. "They're running toward their death. I guess they're heroes." Another thought came to him: "Maybe they just don't understand. Maybe they're stupid!"

The noise of the battle was now far away. The young soldier ran more slowly. He saw a general on horseback. The general and the horse were standing quietly, watching the battle. He came closer. He wanted to speak to the general. He wanted to say, "We've lost the battle! Don't stay here!" He was angry with the general, sitting calmly on his horse. "He's doing nothing!" he thought.

Just then, the general spoke excitedly. "They've stopped them!

We'll beat them now!" He gave a quick order to an officer on horseback, and the officer rode away. The general smiled on the earth like a sun. He happily repeated the same words, "They've stopped them!"

Hearing this, the young soldier hid his face in his hands. He felt like a criminal. He looked back through the trees. He heard gunfire and shouting as the blue soldiers attacked. Then he became angry. "We won!" he thought. "But I did the right thing! The enemy was winning, and I saved myself. The army needs me alive, so I stayed alive. They can't fight with dead soldiers. I was right to run away."

He thought about his comrades who stayed on the battlefield. "They were wrong to stay. They didn't understand the danger. They're all stupid!" But he couldn't forget that they won the battle. Now they were heroes. He hated his comrades, and the war.

"What can I do?" he asked himself. "I can't go back to the camp. They'll punish me because I ran away. They won't understand that I did the right thing. They're all too stupid!"

The young soldier went into a thick wood, away from the sound of gunfire. Soon he heard only his footsteps, and birds singing.

He threw a stone at a bird, and the bird flew up into a tall tree. "That bird is like me," he thought. "It saved itself. It's the natural thing to do. So I did the right thing when I saved myself."

It was quiet and green in the wood, and Henry felt calmer. He came into an open space where the sun was shining through the trees. Suddenly, he stopped and screamed. A dead soldier was sitting with his back against a tree. He was wearing a dirty uniform. It was blue when it was new. But now it was a sad green color. Flies circled around the head and walked on the gray face. The mouth was open. The eyes were the color of a dead fish. "He's looking at me!" thought the young soldier in fear. He slowly walked away, still watching. He became more and more afraid.

Suddenly, he ran. He ran for a long time, looking behind him. "Is that a voice? Are those footsteps?" he asked himself. But the only sound was the wind in the trees.

Chapter 6   "Where's your wound?"

The sun was low in the sky, and the forest was silent. Suddenly, there was a loud crash of cannon fire. Hundreds of rifles began firing. Henry listened, then ran toward the battle. He was surprised at himself. First, he ran away from a battle. Now he was running toward it.

He pushed forward through the thick forest until he reached an open space. From there he could see long gray walls of smoke over the battle lines. The sounds of cannon shook him. The rifle fire rang in his ears. He stood and watched, his eyes wide and his mouth open.

"This sounds like a real battle," he thought. "I've only seen little fights." He laughed at himself and his comrades. "We thought that we were winning the war. We thought we were heroes. But nobody knows our names. Nobody knows what we did. Nobody will read about us in the newspapers. And we thought it was so serious!"

He continued moving forward. The battle was like a big, terrible machine. He moved even closer to it. He wanted to see dead bodies. He climbed over a low stone wall. On the other side, the ground was covered with clothes and rifles. A dead soldier lay with his face hidden in his arm. Four or five others lay close together. A hot sun shone on them. "I don't belong here," thought the young soldier. "This place belongs to them."

He imagined the voices of the dead men. "Go away! Leave us alone!" He hurried past, looking behind him.

He finally came to a road. He could hear shouting now, mixed with gunfire. Far away, he could see many dark soldiers fighting in a cloud of smoke.

A line of wounded men was coming toward him, away from the battle. They walked slowly and painfully. They were crying and cursing. One man had a shoe that was full of blood. He was laughing crazily. A man with a broken arm helped him to walk. A gray-faced soldier walked forward like a machine. He was looking at something far away. His hands were pressed against his wounded side. They were covered in blood.

Two soldiers were carrying a wounded officer. "Be careful!" he said angrily. "You're hurting my leg!" He shouted at the crowd of men on foot. "Move out of the way!" The wounded men cursed him quietly as they moved to the sides of the road. One of the soldiers knocked heavily into the gray-faced soldier as they passed.

Men on horseback rode through the line, carrying messages. Officers shouted, "Clear the way!" Teams of horses pulling cannon pushed the wounded men off the road. There were loud cries of pain and anger from all sides.

The young soldier joined the line of wounded men. A small, thin man walked silently in front of him. He was listening to a tall soldier with a beard. The tall soldier was telling the story of the last great battle. The thin man listened to every word. His eyes were wide and his mouth hung open.

The bearded man looked at the thin man and laughed. "Shut your mouth, boy!" he said loudly. "Or you'll catch flies!" The other soldiers laughed.

The thin man moved back beside Henry. His face was red. He looked at Henry shyly, but did not speak. His eyes asked the young soldier to be his friend. He was dirty from head to foot, and there was blood on his uniform. On his head was an old piece of cloth covered in blood. A broken arm hung at his side. Finally, he spoke in a soft voice. "It was a good fight, wasn't it?"

Henry's mind was far away. "Yes," he said impatiently. He walked faster.

The thin man tried to follow him. He wanted to talk to someone. He continued shyly: "Yes, sir! That's the best fight I've ever seen. Those boys didn't run when they heard the guns. No, sir! They stayed and fought! You can't beat those boys!" He smiled at Henry, but Henry said nothing. After a time, he spoke again. "Where were you hit?" Henry just looked at him. He didn't understand.

"Where were you shot?" he repeated. "Where's your wound?"

The young soldier didn't answer. "I-I . . ." His face was red and he looked nervously around him. He turned away suddenly and disappeared into the crowd. The thin man looked after him in surprise.

The young soldier moved back until he couldn't see the thin man. Then he started to walk in line with the others. There were wounds all around him. He thought about the thin man's question and he began to worry. He looked at the other soldiers. "They're all looking at me," he thought. "They know my secret. They can see that I'm not hurt." He began to feel angry. "Everyone thinks they're brave. But they're only wounded! They're lucky!" He too wanted a wound, a red badge of courage.

Then he looked at the gray-faced soldier walking at his side. He suddenly felt bad. "He has a real wound," he said to himself. "I don't belong here."

There were soldiers all around the gray-faced soldier. They spoke to him, but he didn't reply. He walked straight on, looking at something far away. They tried to help him, but he waved them away with his hand. The young soldier looked at the hand again. He gave a cry of surprise. He ran forward on legs that suddenly felt weak. He took the gray-faced soldier by the arm. "Jim!" he screamed.

The tall soldier gave a little smile. "Hello, Henry," he said.

*He started to walk in line with the others. There were wounds
all around him.*

Henry didn't know what to say. "Oh, Jim! Oh, Jim!" he repeated.

The tall soldier held out his hand. It was covered in old, black blood and new, red blood. "Where have you been, Henry?" he asked. "I was worried. I thought that you were dead."

Henry felt worse and worse. "Oh, Jim!" he said again.

The tall soldier continued, "You know, I was out there. It was a terrible fight. And they shot me." He looked surprised. "That's right. They shot me." He shook his head slowly.

Chapter 7   "Leave me alone!"

The other soldiers left Henry alone with his friend. They all had wounds. Suddenly, the young soldier saw a look of fear on Jim's face. The tall soldier held his arm tightly. He spoke in a shaking voice. "I'm afraid, Henry. I'm afraid that I'll fall. And if I fall, the cannon will run over me! Help me, Henry! Please!"

"I'll look after you, Jim!" he cried. There were tears in his eyes.

"I've always been a good friend, haven't I?" asked the tall soldier. "You'll help me, won't you? Just pull me out of the way, that's all." He waited for a reply. Henry made a sign with his head. He was crying now.

But then the tall soldier dropped Henry's arm. He seemed to forget all his fears. He walked carefully along the middle of the road. Henry ran to help him. "No, no, leave me alone," he said in a weak voice. He was looking at a faraway place. Henry followed, wanting to help.

Soon he heard a voice behind him. Turning around, he saw the thin man. "Take him off the road, my friend," he said softly. "The cannon are coming, and they're coming fast. He's going to die. You know that, don't you?"

"Jim! Jim!" cried the young soldier, running forward. "Come with me!"

The tall soldier looked at him, not understanding. Then he seemed to wake up. "Oh! Into the fields?" He walked into the grass.

Henry turned around as the horses passed with the cannon. Then he heard a loud cry from the thin man, "Look! He's running!"

The tall soldier was running across the field, almost falling. Henry felt a sharp pain in his heart as he watched him. He and the thin man began to run after the tall soldier. It was a strange race.

"Where are you going, Jim? Stop! You'll hurt yourself!" called the young soldier. "Jim!"

The tall soldier stopped and turned around. His eyes were sad. "Leave me alone!" he said quietly. "Please!" He continued on his way, almost falling again. The two soldiers followed, watching. At last, they saw him stop. His face was calm. He was in the place that he was looking for. He stood with his arms at his sides. He was waiting for something to happen. Suddenly, his chest began to move in and out as he tried to take in some air. His chest moved faster and faster. With every movement, the young soldier felt the tall soldier's pain.

"Jim!" he cried.

The tall soldier spoke one last time. "Leave—me—alone! Don't—touch me!"

He stood up very straight and his arms shook. Then his legs began a terrible dance. Then his body fell forward. His shoulder hit the ground, and he stopped moving. As his coat fell open, the young soldier saw the terrible wound in his side. He turned away, suddenly angry. He looked toward the battlefield and cursed. The sun was red and angry in the sky.

The thin man stood looking at the body of the tall soldier. "He was a strong man, wasn't he?" he said. "I never saw a man die like that."

The young soldier wasn't listening. He sat on the ground with his face in his hands. He couldn't speak.

"We have to leave him here and go."

The thin man continued: "Listen to me, my friend." He was still looking at the body. "He's gone, isn't he? He's finished. But we're still here. We have to leave him here and go." He was quiet for a minute. "And I'm not in very good health," he added softly.

The young soldier jumped up. "Not you too!" he cried. "You're not going too!"

The thin man waved his hand. "No, no, of course not. I just want some soup and a good bed. Then I'll be all right again. Now let's go!" They looked at the body one more time, then turned away.

They walked silently back onto the road. After some time, the thin man spoke again. "I'm feeling bad now, really bad." His legs were shaking and his skin looked blue.

"Oh, no!" cried the young soldier. He imagined another meeting with death.

His comrade waved his hand again. "I'm not going to die yet," he said. "I can't die. I have too many children and they all need me." He gave a little smile. Henry understood that he was joking. "And when I die," he added, "I won't die like that other soldier. I'll just lie down on the ground."

Henry walked faster, but the other man stayed beside him.

"I know a man named Tom," the thin man continued. "He lives next door to me at home. We're good friends. Well, we were fighting this afternoon. He started shouting and cursing at me.

"'Look!' he shouted. 'You're wounded in the head!'

"I touched my head. He was right. There was blood on my hand. I started running, but just then another bullet hit me in the arm. It turned me right around. So that's why I'm here. It's because of my friend Tom."

He was quiet for some time, then he spoke again. "I can't walk much longer. It hurts too much." He looked at Henry. "You know, you look tired. You should look after yourself. Maybe your wound is getting worse. Maybe it's inside your body. They're the worst. Where is it?" He didn't wait for an answer.

"I had another friend named John," continued the thin man. "He had a wound in the head.

"'Are you all right, John?' everyone asked him.

"'Yes, I'm fine,' he said. 'It's nothing.'

"And the next minute he was as dead as a stone. So you should be careful of your wound. Maybe it's worse than you think. Now tell me, where is it?"

The young soldier didn't want to talk about wounds. "Leave me alone!" he said coldly.

The thin man looked at him sadly. "What's wrong? I didn't do anything."

Henry hated the thin man. "He's trying to learn my secret!" he thought. "Goodbye!" he said in a hard voice.

"Where are you going, my friend?" asked the thin man. His voice was weak. "Don't go away. You're hurt. I'll look after you. Just tell me one thing. Where's your wound?" He walked into the field, talking to himself.

The young soldier quickly walked away. The thin man's question hurt him too much. "I can't keep my secret," he thought. "Everyone will know about my crime, and they'll punish me. I want to die. Then I'll be free."

Chapter 8   "Don't try to stop me!"

The battle sounds were growing louder. The young soldier went around a little hill. The road was blocked with horses and cannon. They were leaving the battlefield. Men were pulling at the horses' heads and hitting them with sticks. A cannon with a broken wheel lay on its side. He heard shouted orders and curses. There was fear everywhere.

The young soldier was strangely pleased. "They're all running away from the battle. They're smart, like me. I did the right thing

28

when I ran away." He sat down to watch. He saw a line of foot soldiers marching quickly toward the battle. The men at the front used their rifles to push through the crowd. The others followed. "Move out of the way!" cried the officers importantly. They were marching proudly, with their heads high. They were going into the heart of the battle.

The young soldier watched them pass. His old fears returned. "Look at them! Where do they find their courage? They're heroes. I'll never be like them. They're marching straight on to their death, and they're not scared. And I'm scared of everything!"

He wanted to change places with one of these heroes. A beautiful picture came into his mind, like a dream. He closed his eyes. He was holding a broken sword high in the air. He gave the order to attack. His comrades followed him, shouting excitedly. He stood alone against the enemy. All eyes were watching as he died for his country. He was a hero.

Henry opened his eyes and jumped to his feet. He was ready to fight again. His country needed him. But then he suddenly felt a little less brave. "How can I fight?" he asked himself. "I don't have a rifle. I can't fight with my hands. And I don't know where my regiment is." He thought about his regiment. "I can't go back," he told himself. "They'll ask too many questions!" He found a new reason. "And I'm sick!" His mouth was burning and his head was on fire. His eyes hurt. His stomach was empty and aching. He began to hate himself because he was weak. "I'll never be a hero!" he thought.

A new idea came to him. "If we lose this battle, even the brave men will run away. Nobody will know that I wasn't brave. Or they'll think that I was smart to run away." He thought again. No, he didn't want the blue army to lose. It was a selfish idea.

He had to return to his regiment, but he was afraid. "What will they say?" he asked himself. He had to think of a story. "But will they believe me?" He was very worried.

He imagined that he was back in the camp. Laughing men pointed at him. "There's Henry! He's scared of his own shadow! Run, Henry!" He had nowhere to hide. He was a joke.

A crash of cannon fire woke the young soldier from his bad dream. Dark waves of men ran out of the woods and down through the fields. They were dropping their rifles and their coats as they ran.

Henry forgot his troubles. The fight was lost. War, the greedy red animal, was coming nearer. It was hungry and it was ready to eat the army. Soon, there were running men everywhere. "What's the matter? Where are you going?" he cried. Nobody saw him, and nobody heard his question. He pulled at a man's arm to stop him. They stood face to face. He tried to speak: "Why—Why?" The man pulled away, shouting, "Don't try to stop me! I have to go!" The young soldier held on more tightly. The man pulled harder. His face was red and angry. "I have to go!" he shouted again. He lifted his rifle above his head and hit Henry hard on the head. Henry's fingers became weak, and he dropped the man's arm. Bright lights danced in front of his eyes and cannon crashed inside his head. The man ran away.

He fell to his knees. Then he tried to get up, fighting against the pain. He got onto his hands and knees. He slowly pushed himself to his feet, like a baby trying to walk. He held his head in his hands and walked slowly across the grass. He touched the wound carefully. Sharp pains shot through his head. His hand was covered in bright, red blood. He looked at it for a long time, then he started walking again. He was afraid to move quickly because of the pain.

He turned onto the road. A young officer on a horse almost ran over him. More men on horseback followed quickly. Then came the foot soldiers. Officers shouted at them as they marched in a long line. At the end came more horses, pulling cannon behind them. The young soldier walked carefully past them along the side of the road.

"Don't try to stop me!"

There were long purple shadows in the forest, and the red sun was going down behind a cloud. The road was now empty. He passed the bodies of horses and broken war machines. His head felt very big, but it didn't hurt now. He began to worry. When he felt the pain, he could measure the danger. He knew that he was still alive. Now he felt nothing. It was worse than the pain.

He thought about the time when he was a boy. He saw his mother cooking in the kitchen. There was a warm light all around her. His dinner was on the table. He remembered swimming in the river. He was laughing with his friends. The water was fresh, and there was a soft wind in the trees.

He grew very tired, and his head hung down. His feet were heavy. He wanted to lie down and sleep, but he was afraid to stop. It was getting darker.

At last, he heard a friendly voice near his shoulder. "You don't look very well, boy!" The young soldier didn't look up. He tried to speak, but his tongue was thick in his mouth. The man took him by the arm. "I'm going the same way as you. I can help you." The man questioned Henry as they went along. He also answered when the young soldier said nothing.

"What regiment are you in? The 304th? They weren't fighting today. They were? Everyone was fighting. I was lost. I didn't know where I was. How did you get here? I guess you fought with another regiment. But we'll find yours. They're a long way from here. Don't worry, we'll find them."

The friendly voice stayed with Henry. They walked through the trees and past the guards. He felt like a child. Finally, they stopped. The friendly man laughed. "Do you see that?" he asked. He pointed to a fire. "That's your regiment. Goodbye and good luck." He shook Henry's hand and walked away.

"He's gone," thought Henry, "and I never saw his face."

Chapter 9   "I'll look after you"

The young soldier walked slowly toward the fire. He was still afraid of his comrades' questions. He thought about hiding in the forest, but he was too tired. Suddenly, he saw a big, black shadow in front of him. It was pointing a rifle at him. "Stop!" called a nervous voice.

Henry stopped in surprise. "Hello, Wilson," he said. "You're here."

The loud soldier came slowly forward. "Is that you, Henry? You're alive! I'm so glad to see you!"

"Yes, it's me," said Henry. He felt weak. He had to tell his story quickly. "I was lost and I couldn't find the regiment. I was far from here, on the right. There was bad fighting. It was terrible. I was shot in the head."

"Why didn't you tell me?" cried his friend. "Come here, Henry. I'll look after you." He put his arm around Henry's shoulders. They sat down next to the fire. Wilson looked at the wound in the firelight. He touched it carefully. "That's it," he said. "A bullet just touched you on the side of the head. It looks like somebody hit you with a stick. You'll be all right, but it's going to hurt tomorrow morning. Wait here. I'll come back in a minute."

Wilson left Henry by the fire. Henry looked around and saw soldiers lying asleep everywhere. They talked in their sleep, and changed from one position to another. An officer was sleeping with his back against a tree. His sword was still in his hand.

Wilson returned with water and coffee. "Here, drink this," he said. The coffee was cold and delicious in Henry's mouth. Wilson wet a cloth and tied it carefully around Henry's head. Henry looked at him gratefully. The cloth was cold on his aching head. "You're a good man, Henry," Wilson said. "Most people scream when they're hurt. But you didn't make a sound." Henry looked

Henry lifted his head weakly. "But this is your bed," he said.

at the ground, saying nothing. "Now lie down and sleep," said Wilson.

Henry lifted his head weakly. "But this is your bed," he said. "Where will you sleep?"

"Go to sleep!" ordered Wilson. "I'll be all right."

The young soldier was already asleep, safe and warm.

He woke up before the sun came up. He was cold and wet. His comrades still slept on the ground like dead men. Wilson was putting more wood onto the fire. "How are you feeling, Henry?" he asked kindly. "Let's see your head." He lifted up the piece of cloth.

"Be careful!" said Henry sharply. "You're hurting me!"

"Come and have something to eat now," said Wilson patiently. "Then you'll feel better." He brought Henry some coffee, and he quickly cooked some meat over the fire. He sat down and happily watched Henry eat.

Henry was looking at Wilson too. "What happened to him?" he asked himself. "He's changed. Before, he was angry all the time, and he was so proud of himself. Now he's calm. I'm glad that he's changed."

Wilson was thinking about the next battle. "Do you think we'll beat them?" he asked Henry.

The young soldier thought for a minute, then laughed. "Two days ago, you wanted to beat the enemy army alone!"

Wilson looked a little surprised. "Did I?" he asked. "I guess I was stupid then. Maybe I've changed. The officers say we're beating them."

"I don't know about that," the young soldier replied. "Yesterday I thought they were beating us." Henry suddenly remembered something. "Jim Conklin's dead. He was shot in the side."

Wilson looked at him in surprise. "No! Poor old Jim!" He looked silently into the fire.

There were other small fires all around them. Groups of men sat drinking coffee and talking. One man stood up suddenly and dropped a cup of hot coffee. It fell on another man's knee. There was loud shouting and cursing.

"There's going to be a fight!" said Wilson. "I'm going to stop them." He went to the angry men. "Now, boys," he said quietly. "Don't fight. Fight against the enemy, not against your friends!"

All three men were talking excitedly and waving their arms. Finally, the two men sat down and Wilson came back. "I have to fight one of them after the battle," he said calmly. "He didn't like what I said."

The young soldier laughed. "You've really changed," he said.

Wilson didn't reply. He was thinking. Finally, he spoke. "You know, we lost over half the men yesterday. But they weren't all dead. They were lost, that's all. They were fighting with other regiments. Just like you." The young soldier said nothing.

Soon the regiment was standing on the road. They were waiting for the order to march. Henry put his hand into his pocket. "What's that?" he asked himself. He pulled out a yellow envelope. Then he remembered. "Wilson's letters," he thought in surprise. He almost spoke to Wilson, but he changed his mind. He decided to wait. "Wilson was scared when he gave me those letters," he thought. "If he asks me any questions, I'll talk about the letters. He'll remember his fear, then he'll stop asking questions." He felt a little sorry for his friend. "Poor old Wilson," he thought, "crying like a baby."

He thought about what happened the day before. He forgot his own fears. He was really quite pleased with himself. "I ran away from the battle, but nobody knows about it," he thought. "And I did it for a good reason. The other men ran away because they were afraid. I ran away because I was smart."

He wasn't worried about the future. "I can do the same thing again if I have to," he told himself. "With a little luck, nobody will know." Now he felt sorry for his comrades. They didn't understand.

Just then, Wilson spoke. "Henry."

"What?"

Wilson was looking at the ground. "I-I guess I'll take back those letters." His face was red.

Henry slowly took the envelope out of his pocket. He wanted to say something, because Wilson was so weak and afraid. Finally, he decided to be kind. "Here they are, Wilson," he said. As he watched his friend suffer, he felt even stronger and braver.

Chapter 10   "They fight like cowboys!"

The young soldier's regiment stopped near a wood. They lay on the ground behind piles of earth and waited for their turn to fight. Some men put their heads down and slept. The sound of rifle and cannon fire was everywhere, but they couldn't see the battle through the trees. The men were unhappy. "What are we waiting for? Why don't we do something?" they asked.

The noise got louder, then stopped. The men called, "What's happening?"

Answers came from all sides. "We're losing! They're beating us!" The rifle fire grew louder. Soon they were marching away from the woods. They heard the enemy behind them, shouting.

Henry was angry. "Why are we going back?" he asked loudly. "We were fighting well, and now they're telling us to leave. Those generals are stupid."

His friend replied sadly, "We're going back because they beat us. It's just bad luck."

The young soldier continued: "But it's not fair! We fight as hard as we can." Henry suddenly felt surprised. "Did I say that?" he asked himself. He looked around him nervously. The other men weren't listening. This gave him the courage to continue. He repeated something that he heard that morning. "The general says that we're the best new regiment. So if we lose, we can't help it."

"I guess so," his friend agreed. "Our boys try hard."

"That's right!" said Henry. "We're not losing because of them. We're losing because of those stupid generals! They don't know what they're doing. We fight hard every time, but we can't win."

A man spoke beside him. "What do you know? Were you the only one who was fighting yesterday?"

The question was like a knife in his heart. "No," he said quickly. "Of course not."

Henry stopped talking. He looked at the other men. "They stayed and fought," he thought. "Do they know that I ran away?" He walked along silently.

They heard firing behind them. Sometimes it seemed close, and then it was far away again. The men looked behind them angrily. Finally, the regiment stopped in an open space between the trees. The men formed into battle lines and turned to face the enemy. As the sound of rifles became louder, the sun came up.

"I knew it!" said an officer angrily. "They waited until the sun came up! Now they're going to attack!" He stood behind his men and pulled at his mustache.

A line of cannon fired shells toward the enemy. The regiment lay on the ground and watched the shadows in the woods.

"I'm tired of this!' said the young soldier angrily. "We march from one place to another. We don't know where we're going. We fight hard but they beat us. Why did we come here? Nobody knows. And now we have to fight again."

Wilson looked tired, but he answered his friend calmly. "Don't worry. Everything will be all right."

"Don't tell me that!" replied the young soldier. "I know . . ."

A loud voice spoke behind him. "There's too much talking

and not enough fighting in this war!" It was an officer, and he was angry.

The noises of battle were coming nearer. One rifle fired at the regiment, then many more. Cannon fire crashed behind them. More cannon answered in front of them. The tired men lay waiting for the attack. There was no escape. The shouts of the enemy became louder. The men turned and waited.

Henry was angry again. "Why don't they leave us alone? Don't they ever get tired?" He needed to rest and to think. He hated the enemy army.

The regiment fired, all together. A thick wall of smoke blocked their view. Their rifle fire cut through it like knives.

Henry spoke into his friend's ear. "Why are they following us? If they continue, we'll kill them all. Don't they know that?"

His friend had a different idea. "If they continue, they'll push us into the river!"

When he heard this, the young soldier gave an angry shout. He waited behind a little tree. His eyes burned with hate for the enemy. He showed his teeth like a dog.

The enemy fired again. The regiment replied. The young soldier quickly fired from behind the tree. He fired again. "I'm not going to move," he promised himself. His rifle became hot, but he continued firing. Smoke burned his eyes. He gave an angry cry every time he fired. When the enemy moved back, he moved forward immediately. When the enemy pushed them back, he moved back slowly and angrily.

He was still firing when the others stopped. He was lost in his feeling of hate for the enemy. He put down his rifle when he heard, "What's he shooting at? There's nobody there!" His comrades were looking at him in surprise. He looked at the empty field in front of him. "Oh," he said, understanding. He lay on the ground beside his comrades. The battle sounds were still in his ears.

An officer called to the young soldier, "Good work! Give me ten thousand more like you, and I'll win the war in a week!" He looked very pleased with himself.

When Henry's comrades heard this, they looked at him differently. "I didn't know he could fight like that!" they said.

Henry lay on the ground to rest and he thought about the battle. He was proud of himself. "I fought like a hero," he told himself. "And it was easy!" He was pleased that his comrades were watching him.

He listened to the men talking. "The enemy lost a lot of men, didn't they?"

"That's right. And we haven't finished yet! The army will never see another new regiment like us!"

The regiment rested for a time, but the battle continued around them. The men were hot and thirsty. Wilson and Henry went to find some water. As they were returning, they could see the battlefield. On one side, they saw a line of guns in a gray cloud of smoke and fire. On the other side, a long line of soldiers followed a road. Shells passed over their heads, and bullets hit the trees. Wounded men moved slowly through the trees.

A general and another officer on horseback passed the two friends. They listened closely for any news. The general spoke first. "The enemy's going to attack. We have to stop them. We have to attack first. I need more men. Which regiment can you give me?"

The officer thought for a minute. "The 12th are fighting with the 76th," he replied. "But you can have the 304th. I don't need them. They're not very good. They fight like cowboys!"

Henry looked at Wilson in surprise. "The 304th!" he said. "That's us! And he called us 'cowboys!' What does he mean?"

The general spoke again: "Get them ready. I'll send you the order." He began to ride away, then he turned back. "I don't believe that many of your cowboys will return."

"They fight like cowboys!"

Chapter 11   "Give it to me!"

The two friends ran back to the lines. An officer stopped them. "Where have you been?" he asked angrily. He stopped talking when he saw their excited faces.

"We're going to attack!" shouted the young soldier.

"Attack!" said the officer in surprise. "That's real fighting!" He smiled proudly.

The other soldiers stood in a circle around the two friends. "Is it true? Are we going to attack?"

"Yes! It's true!" replied the young soldier. "We heard the general talking!" A few minutes later, the order arrived. The officers quickly pushed the men into line. The regiment stood ready, watching the woods. They could hear the two armies battling all around them.

The young soldier looked at his friend. He thought of the general's words: "not many of your cowboys will return."

They were the only ones who knew this secret. The man beside them spoke in a low voice. "They're going to eat us!" The two friends silently agreed, but their faces showed no fear.

The young soldier watched the woods carefully. From the corner of his eye, he saw an officer on horseback. He was waving his hat. The regiment pushed forward and shouted, then began to run. The young soldier ran like a man followed by wild dogs. His eyes were red, and his face was hard. His uniform was dirty. On his head he wore a blood-covered cloth. His rifle hit his shoulder as he ran. He looked like a madman.

As the regiment moved into an open space, the shooting started. Yellow fire shot out from the trees. The men broke into small groups as they ran into the woods. The enemy shouted as they fired. Shells passed through the trees over their heads. One landed in a group of men and broke into bright red pieces. One of the men threw up his hands to protect his eyes. Other men were hit by bullets. They fell to the ground, screaming. The regiment left them behind. They forgot the danger as they ran madly forward. They shouted their hate at the enemy.

Soon they became tired and they began to run more slowly. Then the regiment stopped and stood with their rifles in their hands. They watched their comrades dying all around them. They watched the enemy stupidly. An officer screamed, "You can't stay here! Move!" He stood with his back to the enemy and cursed them.

The young soldier fell to his knees and fired an angry shot. His comrades woke up and began firing again. They moved carefully from tree to tree. The smoke was thick in the wood. The gunfire became louder as they moved forward.

They slowed down again before an open space. An officer took Henry by the arm. "Move!" he shouted in his ear. "We'll be killed if we stay!" He pulled him forward. Henry shook off the officer's hand.

"You come too!" he shouted back at the officer.

Wilson ran after them. The three men shouted together to the others, "Move! Move!" A soldier ran past them carrying the flag. The regiment followed. They ran with their heads low. They ran into the bullets and the yellow fire. They ran on through thick blue smoke. The noise of the firing filled their heads.

Henry ran with his eyes almost closed. He followed the bright colors of the flag. He loved the flag. He felt proud to fight for it. Suddenly, a bullet hit the soldier who was carrying it. He fell to the ground. Henry and Wilson jumped forward at the same time. They pulled the flag from his dying hands.

The two young soldiers looked behind them, holding the flag. A few men were still shooting. They were facing the enemy, but moving away from the battle. An officer's voice screamed above the noise: "Where are you going? Shoot them!"

The young soldier and his friend both pulled at the flag.

"Give it to me!"

Henry pulled the flag out of Wilson's hands.

"No, let me keep it!"

Henry pulled the flag out of Wilson's hands.

The regiment moved back through the trees to an open space. Rifle fire was coming at them from all sides. The tired men moved more and more slowly. They wanted to give up the fight. It was not possible to win.

The young soldier was angry and unhappy. He thought about the general who called his comrades "cowboys." "I wanted to prove to him that we're good fighters," he thought. "And now we've lost!" He hated the general, and he wanted him to die. He held the flag higher. He shouted at his comrades, and pushed them with his free hand. He and the officer called them by name, but they didn't listen. The regiment was a broken machine.

Suddenly, the smoke lifted, and they saw the enemy all around them. The men cried out in fear. They didn't know which way to run. Henry stood in the middle of the crowd, holding the flag. His friend came to him. "I guess this is goodbye, Henry," he said in a low voice.

"Oh, be quiet!" replied the young soldier. He didn't look at Wilson.

The officers tried to move the men into a circle. A young officer stood holding his sword. He was watching the woods closely. He gave a loud shout. "They're coming!" The regiment fired. They could see the faces of the enemy soldiers. They wore light gray uniforms. Each side angrily returned the other's rifle fire. The smoke grew thicker, but they continued firing.

The gray soldiers came closer. "There's no hope for us," thought Henry sadly. He dropped to the ground and sat with the flag between his knees. He watched his comrades fight. "We're hurting them badly," he told himself.

Then he noticed that the enemy fire was growing weaker. The regiment looked around through the smoke. As the smoke lifted, they saw a battlefield without soldiers. Only the dead were still there. The blue soldiers stood up slowly. Their eyes burned and their faces were dirty, but they were happy. They shook hands and smiled proudly. They felt like real soldiers now.

Chapter 12   "He's wrong!"

Their small corner of the forest was quiet again. There were battle noises far away, but the regiment was out of danger. They started marching back toward their lines. The men were nervous, looking behind them. They were afraid of a bullet in the back. "If I'm going to die, I want to die in battle!" thought the young soldier. "Not like this!"

They passed another regiment. The men were resting under some trees. Their faces were hard and sunburned, and their uniforms were old and dirty. They laughed and called out as the regiment passed.

"Where have you been? Are you coming back already? Where are you going? Home to mother?"

The tired regiment heard this, but they didn't reply. One man wanted to fight. An officer pushed him back into line. The men walked heavily with their heads down. The young soldier looked at the older soldiers with eyes full of hate.

Finally, they got back safely to their line. Henry thought about the battle. He was pleased with his day's work.

As the regiment was resting, a general arrived on a tired horse. "Look!" said Henry to Wilson. "He's the one who called us 'cowboys'!" They listened as he spoke angrily to the officers of the regiment.

"Why did you stop?" he shouted. "Why did you stop fighting?"

"But we went as far as we could!" said one of the officers.

"Well, that wasn't very far, was it?" shouted the general. Now all the men were listening. "Your men aren't even cowboys! They fight like farm boys!" He turned his horse and rode away.

The men were surprised and angry. "Farm boys! He wasn't even there!" they said. "He didn't see us fight! It's all a mistake. He's stupid!"

"Why did he say that?" cried Henry. "We fought hard, didn't we?"

A group of men arrived. "Henry!" called one soldier. "Did you hear the news? I heard two officers talking. One of them asked, 'Who was carrying the flag?' The other said, 'Henry Fleming, and Wilson. They were at the head of the regiment.' And do you know what he said next?"

"What?" said Henry.

"He said, 'Those two are excellent soldiers! They'll be generals one day!'"

Henry and Wilson spoke together. "No, it's not true! You're lying!" They felt shy in front of the others, but they were very happy. They forgot their mistakes and their worries. They silently thanked the two officers for their kind words.

Before long, the enemy poured out of the woods again. Henry felt calm as he looked around him. On one side, two regiments were fighting in a field. On the other side, a blue regiment was attacking the enemy outside a wood. There was a line of cannon behind them. The noise was terrible. He saw small groups fighting close together. Men on horseback moved forward, then back again. Bright flags waved through the smoke. Rifles crashed and men fell to the ground. The young soldier did not know who was winning.

His regiment didn't wait for an order. They fired and fired again. They shouted angrily at the enemy. An officer stood behind them, cursing loudly. A gray line of enemy soldiers ran closer and hid behind a stone wall. Henry held the flag and watched silently.

"That general was wrong!" he thought. "He called the regiment 'cowboys' and 'farm boys.' He'll be sorry when I'm dead!" He imagined his body lying in the field. It was full of bullet wounds, but the flag was still in his hands. The general was crying beside him. It was a hero's death. Then he came out of his dream. His comrades were falling all around him. Men screamed in pain. Wilson was still beside him, and his face was black with smoke. The officer was still cursing, but more quietly now. The rifles fell silent as the regiment grew smaller.

The officers of the regiment ran up behind them. "We have to attack!" they cried angrily. The men ran forward, shouting loudly. The young soldier stayed in front with the flag. He felt no fear as he ran. The bullets could not stop him. He had a clear picture of the battle in his mind as he ran. In this picture, the blue regiment crashed into the enemy and broke it to pieces. But as he came closer, he saw something different. The gray soldiers were running away. A few men turned and fired as they ran. Some of them stayed to fight and fired from behind the wall.

The blue soldiers ran faster, shouting wildly. They were angry with the general. "Cowboys! Farm boys! He's wrong!" shouted one man. "We're good soldiers!" They turned this feeling against the enemy. They showed their teeth like wild animals.

The young soldier didn't look at the men who were firing at him. He saw only the red enemy flag, waving in the smoke. It was a prize that he had to win. Nothing could stop him. The blue soldiers raced on through the bullets. They were very close to the gray line. Suddenly, they stopped and fired. The noise crashed in their ears. The group in gray was broken, but they continued firing. Men fell dying onto the ground. A gray soldier still held the flag. He was badly wounded and in terrible pain. Still, he tried to protect the flag. He held on to it tightly, but he was growing weaker. Henry saw that it was his last battle.

The blue line of soldiers poured over the wall, with Henry and his friend in front. His friend jumped at the red flag like a wildcat. He pulled it free, shouting wildly. He lifted it high above his head. It was the last thing the gray soldier saw. He fell down dead on the green grass in a pool of red blood.

He lifted the flag high above his head.

Chapter 13   "It's finished!"

The last gray soldiers threw down their rifles and sat on the ground. They watched with unhappy faces as the blue soldiers shouted happily. Some of the blue soldiers tried to talk to them. One man didn't look up or reply. A wounded man cursed them loudly. A young gray soldier answered their questions. They talked calmly about marching and fighting. The blue soldiers watched and listened with interest. The enemy was a mystery when he was far away. Now they could see his face and listen to his voice. They saw that he wasn't very different from them. He was an ordinary man.

Henry and Wilson shook hands and smiled happily. They sat together in the long grass, resting. They were still proudly holding the two flags.

The men could still hear the faraway crash of cannon, but the sounds of rifle fire were getting weaker. The young soldier and his friend watched a long line of blue soldiers. They were marching over a hill, with their rifles on their shoulders. Behind them came officers on horseback and horses pulling cannon.

"What now?" Henry asked himself. "Another battle?"

The order came to move. There was loud cursing. They were too tired. They stood up and formed a line. They marched slowly back across the battlefield. As they went into the forest, they joined another regiment.

They passed a big white house. Groups of their comrades lay there with their rifles ready. Cannon fired at the faraway enemy. Enemy shells answered. Horsemen rode along the line.

When they reached the road, they turned toward the river. The young soldier understood. He looked behind him at the battlefield. Bodies were still lying everywhere. He suddenly felt calm. He turned to his friend. "It's finished! We're going back to camp!"

"It's finished!"

Wilson looked back over his shoulder. "You're right," he agreed. "It's finished."

"I'm still alive!" Henry thought happily. "I've been to war, and I've come back." When he was fighting, he didn't have any time to think. Now he remembered everything. "I've done a lot of brave things," he thought proudly. The sun shone and music played in his head. Beautiful pictures passed through his mind.

He heard an officer's voice, "Give me ten thousand more like you, and I'll win the war in a week!"

Then another voice spoke. "Those two are excellent soldiers! They'll be generals one day!" His comrades heard these words and smiled at him. He gave them a little smile. He watched himself running toward the enemy position. He wasn't afraid. He held the flag high, and the rest of the regiment followed him.

He looked into the future. He was at home. His mother and the neighbors were there. He was telling them about his adventures. He was the hero of his stories, and they were listening with wide eyes. He went into town. His friends asked him questions: "What was it like? Tell us, Henry." A girl with dark hair was watching him.

Then, a different kind of picture came into his mind. He wasn't happy to see it, but it stayed with him. The tall soldier stood in front of him. He was holding his side. Blood poured out through his fingers. "Where have you been, Henry?" he asked. "I was worried. I thought that you were dead."

Then he saw the thin man. There was blood on his head, and a bullet hole in his arm. His dying voice was weak. "Don't go away," he said. "You're hurt. I'll look after you."

Then he saw himself running away from the battle. He was looking behind him with fear on his face. But he went back to his regiment with his red badge of courage. He was telling Wilson his story. "I was lost, and I couldn't find the regiment. I was far from here, on the right. It was a terrible fight. I was shot in the head." Henry felt very bad.

He looked nervously at the men marching beside him. "Can they see into my mind?" he asked himself. "Do they know my secret?"

As he marched away from the battlefield, the terrible thoughts stayed with him. "Will they stay with me all my life? I just want to forget them."

Then he grew calmer. "I was brave sometimes," he thought. "I faced death. I was afraid sometimes, but I didn't die of fear." He looked at his comrades with different eyes. "I guess they were afraid, too," he thought. "They're not perfect either. We're all the same." He felt stronger now. He wasn't afraid to look his comrades in the eye. He didn't realize it, but he was now a man.

A light rain fell on the tired soldiers. It washed away their anger and their bad dreams. In Henry's mind, he saw soft, green fields under a blue sky. A little stream ran through a valley. Over the river, the golden sun shone through the gray rain clouds.

ACTIVITIES

Chapters 1–4

Before you read

1 Find these words in your dictionary.

army   bullet   cannon   comrade   hero   regiment   rifle   shell   sword   uniform

Which words describe:

a a person or a group of people?

b something that soldiers wear?

c something that soldiers use?

2 Find these words in your dictionary. Use them to complete the story.

battle   beat   camp   curse   flag   forward   march   wound

The soldiers leave the .... They ..... along a road. A young soldier carries the ...... He is thinking about his first ....., and he is afraid.

Another soldier says, "We're going to ..... the enemy!" The soldiers move ..... slowly into the woods. Suddenly, they hear a shot. An officer is hit in the hand. He begins to ..... angrily. His ..... hurts very badly.

After you read

3 Answer these questions about the story.

a Does Henry's mother want him to join the army? Why (not)?

b What do the soldiers do in the camp?

c One day, the regiment leaves the camp. How does Henry feel at the end of that day? How does the loud soldier feel?

d What do the soldiers carry when they are marching? What do they wear?

e Why does the loud soldier give Henry a yellow envelope?

f How does Henry feel after his first battle?

4 Work with another student. Have this conversation.

Student A: You are Henry. Explain why you want to join the army.

Student B: You are Henry's mother. Explain why you want him to stay at home.

Chapters 5–9

Before you read

5 These are sentences from the next part of the book. What do you think is happening at the time?

    a "They're coming again!"   **d** "Don't try to stop me!"

    b "Where's your wound?"   **e** "I'll look after you."

    c "Leave me alone!"

6 Find these words in your dictionary.

    badge   courage

    What do you think the *red badge of courage* is? Why does Henry want one?

After you read

7 Put these sentences into the right order. Number them.

    a The regiment is resting when the enemy soldiers attack.

    b A soldier hits Henry on the head with his rifle.

    c Henry joins the line of wounded men.

    d Henry drops his rifle and runs away.

    e A friendly soldier helps Henry find his regiment.

    f Henry leaves the thin man alone.

    g Wilson looks after Henry.

    h Henry meets the tall soldier again.

    i Henry and the thin man stay with Jim as he dies.

8 Why does Henry leave the thin man alone? What do you think will happen to the man? Give reasons for your answer.

Chapters 10–13

Before you read

9 When Henry returns to his regiment, he has two secrets. What are they? Will his comrades discover them? Why (not)?

After you read

10 Who says these words? Who is he speaking to? What does he mean?

    a "They fight like cowboys!"   **c** "He's wrong!"

    b "Give it to me!"   **d** "It's finished!"

11 Work with another student. Act out this conversation.

> *Student A:* You are a general. You called the regiment "cowboys" and "farm boys." Explain why you said this.
>
> *Student B:* You are an officer of the 304th regiment. You think that the men fight very well. Explain why you think this.

12 How does Henry feel at the end of the story? How did he act on the battlefield? What do you think of him?

Writing

13 You are Henry. Write two pages in your notebook, one before the battles and one after them. What are you doing? How do you feel?

14 You work for a newspaper. Write a story about the battle where Henry and Wilson take the enemy flag.

15 You are Henry. You were in the camp with Jim Conklin. You marched and fought with him. You were with him when he died. Write a letter to his family about this.

16 This story happens in 1863. What is different about a soldier's life today? What is the same?